FROM MURDER CAPITAL

TO POLICE STATE

The Real Story Behind Camden's

Transition

ANGELA DAVIS

Dedicated to;

My children Ajani, Zuri and Judah. You guys encouraged me and cheered me on every step of the way. I love you with everything in me.

My mother, Ruby Dixon. You taught me to stand and fight for what I know to be right. I miss you dearly.

ACKNOWLEDGEMENTS

I am extremely grateful for all of the help and guidance that my brother, Earl, provided me during the course of these writings. His knowledge of Camden politics, history and inner workings is simply uncanny. The importance of his contribution to this book cannot be overstated. I also want to thank my dear friend and mentor, Robert Rowe. God wisely placed you in my life just before my mother died. You stepped into the role of spiritual father and have remained so ever since. You and Mrs. Rowe have never failed to be there for me and I am grateful for you both.

Copy Right 2014 by Angela Davis

Table of Contents

1. Introduction……………..……..7
2. Camden…………………….…11
3. My Journey………..................15
4. Camden County Jail………....32
5. The Drug Epidemic…….……39
6. Disparity In Drug Laws……...47
7. Profiling………………..…….50
8. Caught Up In A Sweep……….54
9. Exploitation………………..…58
10. Oppression…………………....68
11. Police State……………….......74
12. Prison Industrial Complex……92
13. Prison Reform………………..103
14. A Bright Future…………..….110
15. Business Savy………………...114
16. Notable Residents…………….125
17. Progress………………………132
18. Helping Inmates Transition….134

PROLOGUE

Much of the information that follows is not well known to many in mainstream America. Your worldview about crime, race, poverty, and the criminal justice system may be challenged. As is often the case with new information that disrupts our paradigm there may be some initial resistance, however, the facts are well documented and speaks for itself. I consider it to be a positive development if this book makes you uncomfortable because discomfort is a precursor to change.

INTRODUCTION

Chapter 1

Picture walking out of your house only to be stopped by an official who demands to see your ID. You see a line of black and brown faces showing fear and helplessness as they too have been stopped to be questioned. You've done nothing wrong. You've violated no laws that you can think of. You aren't aware of anything about your demeanor that would cause you to be singled out. Singled out may not be the right term considering lots of other people are being harassed just as much as you are. Wait! The people the next block over are allowed to move freely about without interference. That's because the next block over is another district. Their residents are shaking their head in disgust at such a blatant violation of civil rights while they silently thank God that being just a few feet behind the township line protects them from this nonsense.

This is done on a daily basis. It has gotten to the point that your stomach now turns with just the thought of going outside but, of course there is no way to avoid it. What did you do to deserve this fate? Nothing at all. You simply happen to live in a place and time where this is the accepted way of life.

Imagine sitting on a city bus filled with mostly poor people. Everyone is engaged in conversation and with the happenings of everyday life. Kids are giggling as they look out the window. A middle aged man is complaining a little too loudly about his ex-wife. A young father is telling his 8 year old son how to handle a bully and to stand up for yourself and not be pushed around. The bus driver sits and looks disinterested as another rider shows their monthly transpass. Suddenly, the bus becomes deadly silent. The atmosphere has become filled with fear and trepidation. A young, stern looking officer has boarded the bus. He scans the sea of faces. Several passengers look down in an attempt to avoid his gaze and the bus driver have some sort of exchange. Some type of information is shared. The officer writes down whatever the driver has told him and quickly exits the bus. It's not until the bus pulls a safe distance away from the officer does the passengers exhale and as if on cue begin complaining about the abuse of authority and how "this is not right!" That young father with the 8 year old son is feeling inadequate, embarrassed and hurt. He too had lowered his head in fear never challenging the unspoken and unprovoked threat that had boarded the bus so arrogantly. Yes, it contradicted what he was trying to instill in his son but, at the same time, his son has to learn his place in society so he can survive.

You may have imagined this as some urban center in the Soviet Union during the 1970's. Perhaps you envisioned Cape Town, South Africa during the Apartheid years. You'd be wrong on both counts. These are actual events that have taken place right here in America in Camden, NJ in 2014.

Of course, things didn't get this way overnight. Like most things, there was a gradual process. This new police state was brought about with the seemingly good intentions of stopping the runaway crime and murders in a city that desperately needed the help. Drastic times calls for drastic measures, after all. Former White House Chief of Staff and current Mayor of Chicago Rahm Emanuel said it best, *"you never want a serious crisis to go to waste...what I mean by that is it's an opportunity to do things you think you could not do before."* You couldn't have a more perfect illustration than what's happened in Camden. As I stated before, however, it wasn't always this way.

CAMDEN

Chapter 2

Located just across the bridge from Philadelphia, Camden has long held the dubious honor of being America's poorest city and often, it's murder capital. In 2012, there were 67 murders. With a population of only 77,000 this would be the equivalent of New York city having 5,360 murders, instead of their actual 414 in 2012, in a city of 8,000,000. To sum it up, Camden had more than ten times the homicide rate of New York.

When I was growing up Camden was a great place to live. We had a movie theatre downtown and a drive-in movie on Mt. Ephraim Ave. The skating rink was just a couple of miles down the street. Centerville swimming pool stayed crowded during hot summer days. We'd have neighborhood parties in Camden High Park in Parkside and Stanley Park in the Centerville section of the city. If we had a problem with somebody then you met them after school, at 3pm, for a fistfight, nothing more.

Many believe that our problems started after the riots of 1969 and 1971. At that time, white residents and businesses moved out of the city. Activists, Charles 'Poppy' Sharp and others, did what they could to stop the citys downward spiral, however, this began a decline from which the city never really fully recovered.

We often find ourselves in the media spotlight for all the wrong reasons. I can remember all of the area newsstands quickly running out of the January 20, 1992 issue titled, "Who Could Live Here?" This was to be the first of many critical articles and news stories to come.

Admittedly, crime has been a way of life here, even for some politicians. We've had 3 mayors be incarcerated. Camden's first incarcerated mayor, Angelo Erichetti, was the first of our city's leaders to serve time. Criminal record or not, he remains well loved by many residents. In spite of corruption charges and an arrest in 1980 for taking bribes in a federal sting operation called Abscam, the mention of Mayor Erichetti still brings a smile to the face of

Camdenites. The perception is that everything he did, both legal and illegal, he did to help improve the city. Mayor Erichetti's story was told in the Oscar nominated movie, American Hustle. Mayor Erichetti passed away in May of 2013.

My earliest memory of someone I know being killed in Camden is that of a guy named Slim. I was very young, maybe 8 or 9 years old. He'd always have his bike decked out with decorations and ornaments. He was stabbed to death. Because this was the first murder that involved someone I knew, it really stuck with me.

One of the most notable of violent acts happened on November 20, 1979. It was at the traditional Turkey Game between Camdens two high school football teams: Camden High and Woodrow Wilson. Two rival motorcycle gangs, The Wheels of Soul and The Ghetto Riders, had a shoot out during the game with thousands in attendance. When the melee had ended 8 people had been shot, including a 2 year old child. 37 gang members had been arrested.

MY JOURNEY

Chapter 3

My perspective on life was a little different than that of many kids my age. Thanks to my older brother, Earl, I was acclimated to the civil rights movement and the struggle of urban minorities very early on. He had me listening to Stevie Wonder's singing, *"you might have the cash but you can't cash in your face…we don't want your kind living in here."* Years later, my love of literature led me to the works of, noted author, Richard Wright, among others. I had a very strong sense of social justice.

Having grown up in Camden I was very familiar with both the victims of violence as well as the perpetrators. Consequently, I was introduced to the correctional system very early in life. I had plenty of friends and family who had been incarcerated. Most of the people that I knew who were in the system was there in an attempt to support their family by selling drugs. Being an advocate at heart, it was only natural that I major in Social Work and "save the world" from the devastation that drugs were causing in our community.

It seems that this tendency to help inmates and other at risk populations runs in my family. My dad, Dr. Earl Dixon, has helped organize and run several programs in Camden through the years. Among his many projects is New Visions Community Services which provides assistance to Camdens homeless population. He conceived and developed the Morgan Village Middle School Longitudinal Program which provided mentoring and tutoring services to city children. Perhaps the most well known of his organizations is Camden Lutheran Housing Incorporated where he served as President for nearly 30 years. This program builds much needed low and moderate income housing for the City of Camden.

I moved out of Camden for the first time in 1993 to live and work in Philadelphia, which is just five minutes away from downtown Camden. I had been living in the family home in Parkside when it suffered damage as a result of a fire that originated in the "hit house" next door. I moved to North Philly, which happened to remind me a lot of Camden. It's funny because people I knew in Philly thought Camden was really dangerous and they wouldnt be caught dead there. My friends and family in Camden thought the same exact thing about Philly. I eventually returned to Camden in 2000.

In actuality, there are a lot of similarities: crime, poverty, being overcrowded and the usual problems of any innercity. Camden, however, has all the big city problems of Philadelphia without any of the advantages. We dont have movie theatres. No public swimming pools. At that time, we didn't have any skating rings. More importantly, we have a very small and still dwindling tax base.

You add to that a huge problem of drug use and the work hazards of being in the drug game, of course it's a recipe for disaster. It's not easy being so stigmatized that other stigmatized cities look down on you. When we were young and in school we thought it was cool to be from Camden because you were thought of as tough. Being an adult from Camden meant being acutely aware that people automatically assumed that you were: violent, a criminal, a drug user and possibly a dealer, and unintelligent. I have had people's entire demeanor change once they knew that Camden was my hometown. It didn't matter that just minutes before we had been conversing and speaking to each other as intelligent, law abiding equals, giving each other mutual respect.

I began volunteering at the Pennsylvania Prison Society. This group has been advocating for prisoner's rights since 1787. It was my job to investigate prisoner's allegations of mistreatment as well as advocate for their rights.

A year later, in 1994, I then began working at Greater Philadelphia Center for Community Corrections. It was later renamed Kintock. We were a rapidly growing half way house for both state and federal inmates. I learned so much during this period. I met inmates of every variety and background. I met former mayors, senators, old time gangsters and everything in between. Many of the residents were well to do

I left Kintock to begin working as a Family Preservation Specialist at Division of Youth and Family Services (DYFS) in Camden. It was my job to help parents meet program goals so they could re-gain custody of their children from the state. This was, by far, the most difficult position I have ever had. Seeing babies and children with injuries, burn marks and STDs was too much for me. This was the only job that caused me to have stress related health problems. I left after just nine months.

It was April of 2003. I was working at a partial hospital program for ex-offenders in Philly when I got the call that one of my nephews had been shot. I suddenly felt really hot and then a bit dizzy. After being shot dozens of times, somehow Mookie (known as JB by his friends) had survived. I wasn't sure how God had worked this miracle but I was so glad He did.

I already knew the routine of what to do when visiting gunshot victims in the hospital. I'd had many friends and classmates who ended up in the same trauma unit at Cooper Hospital downtown. The victim always was admitted under a fake name just in case their assailant wanted to try to get to them again. There was a huge host of family members who all wanted to see him. When it was my turn I tried my best not to cry just in case he was awake. He wasn't. He was sleeping because he was heavily sedated.

Days later, without warning, he died. I was totally confused, angry, hurt and scared. I was confused because I thought for sure God had answered our prayers. Why would He allow us to get our hopes up and spend time with Mookie when He knew all along He was going to take him? I was angry because Mookie was one of the good ones. He was a giant teddy bear that everybody loved. He had been a star football player for Woodrow Wilson High in East Camden. He had gone on to college on a football scholarship. He was working and taking care of his wife...so...why him?! I was hurt because I felt that God had truly failed our family. I was raised in the church and up to this point had believed that God never makes mistakes. I knew that there was no way He could actually fail me but in that moment my heart didn't agree. I was scared because my sister, Mookie's mother, had done an excellent job with both of my nephews. She was a dedicated hard working nurse. Divorced years earlier, she saved and bought a home by herself. She attended all of the school events. She monitored the type of friends they associated with. She purposely kept them busy in extra curricular activities. She supported them in every endeavor. In my mind she did everything right. If a mother who does everything right can still have a son murdered on Camden streets...then...who was safe? I went into a depression.

Unlike a lot of murders in Camden, my nephew's murder was not drug related. He was a bouncer at a neighborhood bar. He intervened in a dispute between two bar patrons. One of them threatened my nephew and later made good on his threat.

In December 2004, the following year, another tragedy struck close to home. A three year old toddler was shot in the neck. Her mother was driving in the Centerville section of Camden with her daughter in the back seat when the toddler was hit by a stray bullet. This was so out of the realm of comprehension I was barely able to function. Here again, we have a single mother, working hard and doing everything she is supposed to do. She was driving home after picking up some food from a local store. We all do this. Certainly a mother should be able to drive her baby home after picking up some food without it turning into a life and death struggle.

She attended the same home daycare as my oldest daughter. My daughter's play pal was now struggling to stay alive and resume a normal life at a time when she should have been playing with Elmo. I took a teddy bear to Cooper Hospital to try and visit but I was not on the approved list so I had to leave it with the security guard. I asked the sitter, Mrs. Beverly, to please let toddler's mother know that I was praying for both of them.

As for that beautiful baby girl, my main comfort is that her life has been spared. Last I heard she was receiving physical therapy and making progress. I'm amazed at her mother's strength and tenacity. I know God has great things planned for this beautiful little girl.

I went into a deeper depression after that. I was angry at God and the city that I loved. My newlywed nephew and this beautiful 3 year old baby were not supposed to be added to Camden's statistics. They didn't sign up for this.

I would like to say that I prayed and this heavy veil lifted but that's not what happened. I was angry and depressed and became even more so as time went on. I'm not sure whose prayers brought me through but they weren't mine. I didn't feel much like talking to God during those times but He held me anyway. I had to get myself together because I had kids to raise. I couldn't stay stuck in this angry and depressed state. It wasn't helpful to anybody.

Mercifully, when I calmed down enough to talk to God about these shootings, He indeed spoke back by way of very gentle, calming thoughts. I began to get the sense that He wasn't toying with our family's emotions by having Mookie hang on for a few days only to take him. In His mercy, God was actually allowing us extra time to hug him, kiss him and tell him how much we loved him. I take comfort in the fact that my sister, his mother, had already gone on to be with the Lord when this all played out. She didn't have to have her stomach turn every time she passed the street her baby was gunned down on. I later realized that regardless of how Mookie died, my sister's commitment to her family had paid off. My nephew enjoyed a great life filled with love and laughter. Although it ended far earlier than we could have imagined it was still a full life. Then I look at his little brother, Nate. Again, I see the same good work ethic, sense of responsibility, sober mindedness and love of life that I saw in his big brother. He now has a family of his own and is doing very well in spite of the fact that the family of his childhood is gone. I'm still in awe of the amount of strength and resilience God has provided him.

Somehow God took my hurt and anger and turned it around so that I became even more determined to impact the lives of young people. My nephew was a loving husband. A wonderful son and big brother. A hard worker and a man of faith, he left a great legacy.

Many of our young men are dying on a daily basis without a lot of the opportunities and blessings that Mookie had. I wanted to make sure they knew that there is a God who loves them and has a plan for their lives. This same God cares for them and cares what happens to them. I continue to pray for these inmates until this day.

I began working at Mercer County Correctional Facility just outside of Trenton. As a Mental Health Specialist I helped inmates who had mental health issues. I'd conduct both individual and group counseling. Obtain their mental health history and refer them to the psychiatrist or psychologist if necessary. I'd make the rounds of the jail to make sure that our clients were doing ok. Just like the COs (Corrections Officers) had people to watch, we did too. Little did I know that there was another segment of the jail interested in keeping an eye on what was going on...the gang members.

The gang situation in both the Trenton and Camden was challenging. Thankfully, the Health Services Administrator at Mercer County, Ms. Hundley, taught me that gang members had just as much chance to be successful post incarceration as anyone else. For that reason, they were also entitled to the same level of services and opportunity as anyone else.

The level of organization and control that these gangs exhibited could prove problematic for custody staff. At both Mercer County and Camden County jails, gang leaders would appoint a member to pretend to be suicidal or fake some other mental health event so that they could be placed on Mental Health Unit in order to gain access to attack somebody. Gang members assumed that inmates were using the Mental Health Unit as a way of being protected from the remaining jail population.

There was one particular incident where an inmate came to the Mental Health office at Mercer County Jail nearly hysterical. Somehow a gang member who was sweeping the tier had gotten his family's information and would walk by the inmate reciting his family's address. I can't remember the circumstances that caused this inmate to become a target but clearly his family was now a target too.

While making the rounds to check inmates on suicide watch I stopped at one cell only to have a young man, greatly distressed, run to the door and make some sort of gesture with his hands just beneath his belly button. He was also whispering something in desperation. I was just about to write him up for being inappropriate when I finally understood that he was gesturing the letter "C" for Crip. He was in the medical cell with a known member of the Bloods. At that time, the Bloods outnumbered the Crips by a huge margin in Mercer County. I alerted custody who immediately had the two inmates separated.

In August of 2006, the unthinkable happened at NJ State Prison in Trenton. A gun had been smuggled in to a Bloods gang member in preparation for a planned riot. A letter had been found weeks earlier stating that other guns would be smuggled to more area prisons so that inmates could arm themselves. Thankfully, as my colleague and

I were gathering material to conduct groups on the tier we were warned about all of the events that had taken place. I should add that it was never established that our inmates had been in on the plot.

In March of 2007, a group of Bloods organized and actually did take over D Pod at Mercer County Jail. The inmates were protesting conditions at the dormitory style jail. There was a nine hour stand off which ended with no injuries or loss of life. Five months later I transferred to Camden County Correctional Facility. My transferring to Camden was coincidental to the stand off at the jail. I was so excited at the prospect of working at Camden. It would cut my commute time in half. It was a city in great need. I had made up in my mind that come hail or high water I was going to make a difference. After all, this was my city.

Having just spoken about gang activities, I must also point out that there have been countless times when these young men have looked out for me. Again, this was the case at both jails. At Mercer County an enforcer for the Bloods that I had been meeting with advised me to stay off of a certain unit when its time for his individual session. His reason...the guys on the unit could be rowdy and disrespectful and he did not want me exposed to this. I believe that many of these young men would gravitate towards staff who were a mother figure.

CAMDEN COUNTY JAIL

Chapter 4

I was both excited and disturbed at having transferred to Camden County Jail. I was excited at the thought of reaching people in my home city. The opportunity to impact lives and offer hope in the community was awesome. I was disturbed at the sheer number of people I knew who had somehow ended up in the system. Of the younger inmates, I knew many of their parents. So much hope and potential locked up in one place was disheartening. Then I realized that, eventually, most of these inmates would be released back into the community. This meant that they could begin making changes now to what they think and how they think so that it's just a matter of time before these changes in thought would translate into changes in their lives. For the moment though, they had their work cut out for them.

It was in Camden that I first became familiar with the initials, GSW, short for gunshot wound. There were countless people who came through with this notation in their medical chart. There were also a number of inmates in wheelchairs. Many of these inmates survived a murder attempt on their life but were not able to get away totally unscathed.

There is one woman at Camden Jail who is the ultimate in mother figures. Marsha Smith, is affectionately known as Ms. Marsha. In her role of Director of the Second Chance Program at the jail she has her hand in just about any worthwhile project that would benefit inmates. The program is a drug and alcohol rehabilitation program that offers so much more. In addition to NA and AA meetings Second Chance also offers GED classes, a literacy program, a computer lab, as well as Anger Management classes. Second Chance works closely with NJ Drug Court.

Ms. Marsha's work on behalf of inmates simply can't be quantified. Anything to enrich the lives of inmates and help them do better, she supports. With as much dedication and respect as she shows them, she is just as committed when holding them accountable. Just like any "mother" she does it because she cares and wants them to progress and not come back as so many often do. She has been at the jail since the 1970s. Ms. Marsha has impacted so many lives that space does not allow me to do her justice.

One of Camden County Jail's unsung heroes is Lt. Hilton. Most people have no idea that she was the gatekeeper to all things entertaining and inspirational to enter the jail. It was her work that enabled me to implement improvements and amenities to the jail on behalf of the inmates. It was she who allowed me to bring in noted author and lecturer, Tom Lagana, Co-Author of, "Chicken Soup for the Prisoner's Soul." It was she, with the approval of management, who allowed me to link up with NJ Drug Court (a much more sensible option for drug offenders than expensive and lengthy incarcerations) and Philadelphia Books Through Bars. These programs donated so many books to our inmates that I was able to start a Mental Health Library. Lt. Hilton had been providing these types of opportunities for inmates long before I arrived and I'm sure she continued to do so long after I had left. It's important that former, current and future inmates know that many of things that they enjoy is thanks to her.

There is a younger woman at the jail who happens to be an officer. She does her job and enforces the rules of the facility while retaining that human touch. She cares and it shows. I'll call her Officer Harry. I'd often hear her advising inmates on community resources and reprimanding them in a way that was humorous but sobering. They always gave her much deserved respect. When I was struggling to start the Mental Health Library she was one of the first people to donate books. Of course the books were positive and promoted self improvement. I believe that God strategically places people in just the right location at just the right time to be a help and encouragement to people in need. Both Ms. Marsha and Officer Harry are just such people.

I need to make mention of the fact that there are also many level-minded inmates with a good head on their shoulders that add to the lives of those they encounter. Mr. Abdul immediately comes to mind when I think of positive influences from within the jail itself.

Although he was a fighter from East Camden he went out of his way to keep the peace among inmates, especially the younger men. He would often seek out positive books and material about history, faith and self-improvement to pass along to other inmates. I noticed that some of the rowdiest, rudest and most out of control inmates would conduct themselves much better when Mr. Abdul was around. He did not allow them to descend to a level of behavior that fit the stereotypes that most people had of them. I often told him that he and I were accomplishing the same goals just from opposite sides of the jail wall...helping people get back on track.

Camden Jail is bursting at the seams, overcrowded with inmates, through no fault of it's own. The jail is merely used to house the great number of people that laws, policies, agendas and poor personal choices have forced through it's doors. The jail, along with the prosecutors officer, is taking steps to address the overcrowding issue.

They have hired consulting firm Luminosity to help create and implement changes. It was this firm that helped the County Jail decrease it's numbers to comply with a court order in 2009.

Thankfully, they helped the jail avoid plans to privatize to save money. I was still working at the jail at that time and it was a scary time for many workers. I'm not sure whether or not inmates were aware of how negatively their lives would have been impacted had those plans been made a reality.

According to an August 11, 2014 article in The Courier Post, the county has made it so that the paperwork process for admissions can now be done at the Camden County Police headquarters instead of at the jail. The prosecutors office has added extra staff to process people more quickly. One of the most exciting prospects for is the possibility of New Jersey voters approving an amendment to our constitution that would allow the release of nonviolent offenders unable to pay bail. It is estimated that a decrease in the jail population could save taxpayers $107 for each inmate.

THEDRUG EPIDEMIC

Chapter 5

Camden's location makes for the perfect drug route. It's only 5 minutes from Philly. Two hours from New York. Two hours from Baltimore. Three hours from Connecticut. Our location would make a great site to build a tourist destination but, as in any economic system, if mainstream businesses won't capitalize on Camden's profit making opportunity the underground economy certainly will. This secondary economic system thrives because of the lack of opportunity through legitimate means.

Fear and uncertainty play a huge role in people's decision to use and sell drugs. Fear of not being able to support themselves let alone a family. In today's economy it's scary for even a young suburbanite entering the job market with a degree.

The jobs just aren't there. Consider the challenges faced by the average Camdenite attempting to enter the job market. First, is having a criminal record. Often times, though not always, there's the challenge of a limited education. Next is having transportation issues due to not owning a car and jobs being concentrated in suburban areas. It really is an employer's market. They have the luxury of being very selective in filling vacant positions. It becomes increasingly clear why so many people feel they have no other option but to sell drugs. After all, the streets are always hiring.

The war on drugs have cost almost 1 trillion dollars since its inception more than 30 years ago. It has resulted in more than 45 million arrests. More than 500,000 people are in jail for drug related offenses. According to Michelle Alexander, civil rights lawyer, advocate, legal scholar and author of The New Jim Crow, "More Black men are in prison or jail, on probation or parole than were enslaved in 1850, before the Civil War began."

As if Camden didn't have enough problems to deal with, a dangerous form of getting high rose dramatically and has played a huge part in adding onto the jail population. Referred to as "wet," this drug is wrecking havoc on the streets of not only Camden but also Philly, New York, Washington DC and many other urban areas.

Wet is when formaldehyde or PCP is dissolved in liquid and then cigarettes or marijuana laced cigars are dipped in it and ready to smoke.

It often causes bouts of psychotic-like symptoms such as: hallucinations, violence, paranoia, and a need to strip naked. The stripping happens when users feel very hot and strip to cool down and they are usually sweating profusely. It is not uncommon for people to report having what they describe as out of body experiences. While working at Camden County Jail one inmate, Steve, told me of instances where he had hallucinated having full blown conversations with dogs. He was convicted of multiple murders which were committed while on wet.

One of the most notable traits of someone coming in on wet is their sheer strength. It could easily take 3 or 4 corrections officers to take down one psychotic inmate who is in the midst of an episode. The best way to describe the inmate's physical ability is superhuman strength. Someone on this stuff is oblivious to pain due to the PCP used to help make it.

PCP was once used as an anesthetic for surgery but was discontinued due to its severe side effects. It's not uncommon for users to end up in the ER with broken ribs and other serious injuries sustained while high. What's more, users often can't remember how they sustained the injury or they speak in incoherent sounds and phrases making it extremely difficult for hospital staff to obtain the patient's history or other vital information.

Two summers ago I can recall getting a phone call from someone who is close to my family named Wadir. Although it definitely sounded like his voice he wasn't making any sense. He was making strange sounds, kind of like a siren. I kept calling his name to snap him out of it but he didn't respond.

A family member was with me so I had him listen to the call to make sure it was Wadir. He confirmed that it was. To say that I was concerned would be a gross understatement. I did the only thing I knew to do and that was to head to East Camden with a gallon of milk and try to coax Wadir into drinking it. This is a home remedy that is said to lessen the effects of smoking wet, however, I can't honestly attest to it's effectiveness. Not thirty minutes later, before

I'd even made it to his house, Wadir called me again, speaking normally as if nothing had happened. Worried, I asked if he was ok. He assured me he was and wanted to know why I had asked. He had absolutely no recollection of our earlier conversation.

In 2012 there were two high profile cases, in Camden, of people who murdered children while on wet. The first incident occurred on August 22nd in the Parkside section of the city. A young mother killed her 2 year old son then stabbed herself to death while reportedly on wet. Obviously, this drug causes people to do the unthinkable. A second incident occurred two weeks later, on September 2nd. In this incident a man from the neighborhood was on wet when he slashed the throats of a 6 year old boy and his 12 year old sister. The brave 6 year old died trying to stop the perpetrator from hurting his big sister. Thankfully, she survived the attack. This little hero was taken way too soon.

Wet puts everyone at risk. The danger is not limited to innocent victims who happen to cross the user's path but the user himself is at risk. The chemicals used is known to cause neurological damage and is suspected to have the adverse effects on the body's organs. User's are usually uninsured and the costs have to be absorbed by the taxpayer. Even when a person abstains from using they could still experience symptoms years later. Like so many other things in our community, even one poor choice could potentially continue to cause damage long after the decision was made. Life isn't as forgiving as it used to be.

There seems to be a never-ending supply of new and addictive drugs. According to a CBS News report on July 5, 2014, there were 259 million prescriptions written in 2012 for painkillers from opiates. With America's increasing addiction to prescription meds drug addiction has also increased greatly. Often these pharmaceuticals act as a gateway drug.

Even the treatment for the addiction has become an addiction. Suboxone Therapy and Methadone Maintenance are two examples. There is even a methadone truck that drives around Camden so that those addicted don't have to travel to an actual methadone clinic.

DISPARITY IN DRUG LAWS

Chapter 6

I got into social work, particularly in the correctional system, because I wanted to "save the world." Growing up in Camden, many of the people I knew had ties to the penal system. I was aware of the reasons that most of my friends and family got incarcerated. By and large those reasons were purely for economic survival. Of course, selling and using drugs is a common contributor to our prison population.

Mandatory minimums sought to make sentencing more uniform with no variability. The very fact that we are dealing with human lives means that there will be variability, mitigating circumstances and the need for a case by case review. Like most policies that take away an individual's right to consider all factors as well as potential consequence, this law was rigid, impractical and unforgiving.

In 2010 President Obama took steps to eliminate the disparity in sentencing for crack cocaine versus powder cocaine. Previously, the ratio for crack to powder had been 100:1. It is now changed to 18:1. This meant that a person would need to have 100 times more powder cocaine as crack to get the same mandatory minimum sentences. This new legislation also did away with mandatory minimums for simple crack cocaine possession.

This disparity hit minority communities the hardest. More than 80% of federal prisoners serving crack cocaine sentences are black. According to a Reuters report, dated February 28, 2008, the US incarcerates more people than any other country. Keeping people locked up is financially burdensome to states that are already strapped for cash. This has set the stage for private companies to come in and offer their services to area jails and prisons. The subject of private correctional facilities will be discussed at greater lengths in a later chapter.

PROFILING

Chapter 7

There are a number of people who believe that racial profiling is necessary and even good. Having been the victim of racial profiling, several times, I couldn't disagree more. I can remember the hostility directed towards Camden residents who were simply driving through some neighboring towns. We felt it from both the residents of adjacent towns as well as law enforcement for those towns. You need to keep in mind that officers are the product of their community. I can remember about 20 years ago I was driving down one of the main streets in Camden, Mt. Ephraim Ave. I'll never forget I had just turned left onto Ferry Ave which brought me right into Woodlynne Borough which was just across the street from Camden. In those years, Woodlynne had a reputation of being especially racist. A young white cop came to my car door screaming to the top of his lungs, spit coming out of his mouth. He demanded to see my paperwork. Finally, he stopped yelling long enough for him to say that I sped through the yellow light, which was probably true.

He went to his patrol car and ran my information. This officer came back to my car an entirely different person. Polite, professional behaving as if his tirade a few minutes ago never even happened. Let me interpret what happened during our brief encounter. This officer expected me to be driving without the necessary paperwork or to have a warrant out for my arrest or some such thing. After all, I was black and coming from Camden. The sad truth of the matter is that this has happened to me too many times to count.

In the summer of 1994, Pennsauken Twp announced that police officers would be randomly stopping every third car coming from Camden. Because the vehicle would be coming from Camden drivers did not need to commit any motor vehicle violation. They did not have to be in a stolen car. They did not need to have a cracked tail light. The only criteria to have your vehicle stopped and possibly searched was the outrageous crime of having come from Camden. The strategy was named "Operation Interface." Thankfully, Camden officials and the ACLU were very vocal in their opposition to this blatantly discriminatory proposal. The plan was eventually scrapped.

To get around this, Pennsauken Police simply started parking at the Save A Lot grocery store in Pennsauken that borders Camden. At the beginning of the month they would sit in the parking lot and try to catch anyone with an expired inspection sticker, a cracked windshield or any thing that will allow them to be ticketed. The township needed money after all and who better to get it from than poor people whose main offense is being poor. However, like most plans that are found to be lucrative, the practice of randomly spying on citizens to increase government budgets has spread to mainstream communities by way of license plate readers. Cops no longer have to stop every third car in hopes of getting a hit. Now all that is necessary is for the officer to simply mount his plate reader on his car and it automatically takes the picture of dozens of plates per minute.

CAUGHT UP IN A SWEEP

Chapter 8

Over the years, I've met with several inmates who insist that they were wrongly jailed because they were caught up in a drug sweep. In New Jersey, there are two types of possession charges; Actual or Constructive possession. Actual means the drugs are actually found on the person's body while with constructive possession the drugs only need to be found in the person's vicinity. It can certainly happen that during a drug sweep any number of Camden residents could be near a drug packet. Because they can't determine who the drugs belong to, everyone in the area is charged with possession.

While there is never a shortage of inmates proclaiming their innocence, quite a few of these guys' assertions rang true. I know from personal experience how easy it is for law enforcement to make no distinction between residents who are going about their daily business and those who are engaged in criminal activity. I've been stopped and followed more than once because of the area I was in. Considering the fact that people live in the area in question, often having to walk to their destination, it's very difficult not to be in a known drug hotspot. If I could be stopped or questioned and I'm a female I can only imagine what it must be like for young black and Hispanic men. Racial profiling and making broad drug sweeps that sometimes net even innocent people in the vicinity only adds to constant flow of bodies processed like merchandise through our already overburdened system.

Mr. Ruiz' (not his real name) story bothered me more than most because he's such a soft spoken, elderly man who, according to him, was just outside of his backyard in an alley in East Camden. The Narcs (Narcotics Unit) came through and began rounding up anyone in the vicinity, Mr. Ruiz included. When I met with him at the jail for counseling he was upset and tearful, to say the least, trying to make sense of it all. One common question that many inmates in this situation ask is "why" I didn't dare mention to them that these practices were nothing new and is done routinely in inner cities all over the country. To add insult to injury, several Camden officers have been imprisoned for planting drugs on suspects a few years ago.

The fall out has been immense. In addition to the innocent people arrested many systems were impacted. Of course families were torn apart. Prosecutors had to release scores of inmates who had been arrested by these rogue cops. There is a high probability that among those who were released some were actually guilty. In the name of justice however, prosecutors have to err on the side of caution. The taxpayers were also brought into this as the state has to payout money for the lawsuits that have inevitably followed.

EXPLOITATION

Chapter 9

Often Camden residents are subjugated and exploited by the very people who are in business to help them. For all of our street smarts and wariness, Camdenites are often quick to trust so called professionals without much question. White collar vultures and various special interests seek to take advantage of the city's poor population to line their pockets. I've seen it from a cross variety of sectors. Unscrupulous doctors, lawyers, insurance agents, salesmen and a host of others.

Perhaps the most disheartening of all are the slumlords. These profiteers come into the city and buy properties and often do a just enough maintenance and repairs to pass inspection. Once the tenant has moved in they essentially are at the mercy of the landlord. Getting repairs made is often just a pipe dream. Many times it never happens. What's worse is that many of these property owners get government funds provided by taxpayers and then refuse to maintain decent housing.

There is one case brought to my attention recently that was simply appalling. This city resident has been living in his home for several years. Both he and his upstairs neighbor, had made repeated requests for the landlord to repair a leak that was coming from the upstairs apartment and leaking into the downstairs unit. Over the course of several weeks a hole eventually formed. A small part of the ceiling collapsed into the tub. When they informed the landlord the response was, "why can't you wash up in the sink?" A day or two later the entire ceiling collapsed. Both tenants could clearly see into each other's bathrooms.

For years landlords have gotten money from the government and/or their tenants and refused to use those funds towards the upkeep and maintenance of their property. According to an article in NJ Spotlight dated April 8, 2014, the costs to rehabilitate the average vacant property in Camden is $100,000. There is little likelihood of city landlords being able to spend any where near that amount. The article went on to say that substandard housing can negatively impact people's health due to mold and rats.

Not only can resident's physical health be compromised, their mental health can be as well. It is stressful to constantly worry that your food, clothes or furniture is infested with pests. There is a particular complex in Camden where the apartments are so over-run with mice that mothers can't put their babies on the floor. They also have a roach and waterbug problem that seems to go unabated regardless of extermination efforts. Some landlords provide fail to provide even that much.

These conventional pesticides that are being sprayed month after month are also having a negative effect on people's health, especially children because their little systems are still developing. Many of the city's children are now fighting respiratory illnesses such as asthma and bronchitis.

I encourage parents to use more natural and alternative methods of pest control that is not harmful to them and their family and is also environmentally friendly. Years ago I began using powdered microalgae and I saw amazing results. We haven't had to use the services of an exterminator in years now. I've shared it with family and friends and they report the same results that I have. It's very empowering for struggling parents to have access to a natural product that enables them to be rid of roaches and even bedbugs at very low economic and environmental cost. Until landlords begin providing a pest free environment as they are mandated to do, then it is up to us to see to it that our loved ones are safe from pests and infestations.

Another way that landlords are exploiting Camden's poor is by way of illegal evictions. It's ridiculous the number of cases I've heard where tenants who were facing eviction went to Camden County Board of Social Services and received an emergency voucher to pay back rent and avoid eviction. On the voucher it states very plainly that the landlord agrees to drop all eviction proceedings once they accept funding from Emergency Assistance. If they don't agree to this then of course no voucher would be issued. The county does this to ensure that resources aren't wasted. In fact, once a person receives a voucher for back rent they are not allowed to receive another one, ever.

What's been happening is that these slumlords are cashing the vouchers and then illegally filing an eviction against the tenant. Most residents are unaware of their rights and they don't fight it because they don't know that they can. Not only have these landlords breached their contract with Emergency Assistance, they have also broken state laws by filing an illegal eviction based on false statements. It is unknown how many taxpayer dollars have been wasted due to this abuse that goes unchecked. Absolutely nothing happens to the landlord and they are free to victimize again as soon as the opportunity presents itself.

The county must do more to recoup these losses and to hold these criminals accountable. This is tantamount to fraud and theft by deception. While researching the subject I saw case after case of landlords and property owners having been prosecuted for such crimes. Not so in Camden. What makes these practices a crime in one city or township yet not a crime when it comes to Camden's poor?

As municipalities all across New Jersey are tightening their belts and adjusting to shrinking budgets…wouldn't it make much more sense to incorporate language right into the voucher that states if a landlord attempts an illegal eviction within 60 days of accepting the voucher, they have to pay the full amount of the voucher back as well as an additional fine. If the landlord commits a second offense the same rules would apply but also charges would be filed against them and they would become ineligible for any further government funding. I think we would see a sharp fall off on these illegal evictions which steal from the poor and give to the rich.

There is good news in all of this. There are agencies in NJ that are fighting for the housing rights of the poor, many of whom have been doing so for a long time. New Jersey Tenants Organization (NJTO) http://www.njto.org/ ,(201)342-3775, has been fighting for the rights of NJ tenants since 1969. In fact, most of the laws that have established tenants' rights in NJ is a direct result of their efforts. While the majority of their work is done at the legislative level they also help individual members. I have personally used laws that NJTO got passed to successfully fight an illegal eviction. I didn't even have an attorney at the time because I couldn't afford one but because I had knowledge of these laws, the judge ruled in my favor.

I've also been able to help other families stay in their homes, as well, based on the work of NJTO. This organization also helps residents organize tenants associations too.

Another organization that is a great online resource for NJ tenants is www.lsnjlaw.org, (888)LSNJ-LAW…(888)576-5529. The tenants' rights handbook was developed by New Jersey Legal Services, sometimes called Legal Aid. They offer free legal advice to New Jersey's poor. Where NJTO got the laws passed for New Jersey's tenants, Legal Aid, interpreted what those laws meant, made it easily available to people and also provided free legal advice and, if necessary, representation.

Fair Share Housing http://fairsharehousing.org/ , (856)665-5444, was formed in 1975 and created the Mount Laurel Doctrine which prohibits economic discrimination against the poor by the state. In an effort to end exclusionary and discriminatory housing patterns, Fair Share Housing makes sure that when new housing is built in NJ a certain percentage is set aside for the poor. Today, they continue to fight to defend the rights of NJ's poor by monitoring, enforcing and expanding the Mount Laurel Doctrine.

Most recently, Fair Share Housing, along with the NAACP and the Latino Action Network reached a settlement in a complaint against the Department of Housing and Urban Development (HUD). They had sued to make more money available to low income renters who were impacted by Hurricane Sandy. Some of these renters may have previously been found ineligible. Homeowners were not the only residents who lost their life possessions and had to start all over. Fair Share Housing, once again, made sure that New Jersey laws were extended to benefit the state's poor just as much as anyone else.

Thanks to the efforts of organizations like these NJ actually has some of the most progressive tenants' rights laws in the country. Sadly, most tenants in Camden and other townships are totally unaware of this fact. I've partnered with other concerned citizens and social justice groups and have begun to lecture to teach residents what their rights are and how to fight any attempts to infringe on those rights. Knowledge really is power.

OPPRESSION

Chapter 10

What is happening in Camden is happening all over the country but not yet to the extent that it exists in Camden. The systematic erosion of our civil rights is being done bit by bit, albeit, at an accelerated pace. The rest of American should not rest comfortably thinking this is a Camden problem. Power out of control always seeks to bring even more under it's control.

Oppression is defined as "prolonged cruel or unjust treatment or control." Using this definition, we could certainly say that America's minorities and it's poor are living under oppression. Noted author, speaker and civil rights lawyer, Michelle Alexander was brutally honest in her description of what is happening in our country in her book "The New Jim Crow." She very accurately explains how society has substituted politically correct labels, mainly that of criminal, to discriminate against people instead of the same old derogatory, racial epithets used in the past. In the end, however, it garners the same racist results. "

Once you're labeled a felon, the old forms of discrimination— employment discrimination, housing discrimination, denial of the right to vote, denial of educational opportunity, denial of food stamps and other public benefits, and exclusion from jury service— are suddenly legal. As a criminal, you have scarcely more rights, and arguably less respect, than a black man living in Alabama at the height of Jim Crow. We have not ended racial caste in America; we have merely redesigned it." – Michelle Alexander (Author of The New Jim Crow)

Historically, whenever those in power wanted to oppress a group of people, they would simply design laws targeting that group. The rights of millions of minority inmates have been effectively trampled on. Their right to vote has been hijacked by way of discriminatory laws.

Secretary of State, John Kerry, while describing elections in Syria stated, *"They are meaningless because you can't have an election where millions of your people don't even have the ability to vote."* http://www.bloomberg.com/news/2014-06-04/u-s-must-accept-presidential-vote-result-syrian-minister-says.html Well said! I am in total agreement. Having said that, how is it possible that here in our own country we currently have 2 million people incarcerated many of whom have lost their right to vote among other things. Additionally, they have also lost their right to subsidized housing. In fact, family and friends with subsidized housing who take them in are at risk for losing their subsidy. I have been practicing social work for more than 20 years and one of the very first things that a Case Manager or Clinician would ask a client is, "do you have any support system?" A support system, as the name would suggest, is anyone (family, friends, peers) who can provide the client with support/help. This resource is immediately taken away, or at least greatly hampered by laws that seek to punish the person who provides help with the most basic of needs…housing. People with drug convictions also lose their right to apply for welfare benefits as well as financial aid. This is an outright blatant, and sorry to say, successful attempt to isolate minorities, the vast majority of whom have drug offenses, so they have no choice but to return to drug dealing and thereby return to jail to continue to provide slave labor to special interests in the correctional system.

It is human nature for people to do whatever is necessary to survive. People resort to whatever means is necessary to feed themselves and their family. American Investigative Journalist, Alfred Henry Lewis said, *" There are only nine meals between mankind and anarchy."* He further said, *"It may be taken as axiomatic that a starving man is never a good citizen."* He accurately surmised that after about 3 days of missed meals people's observance of laws and social norms begin to disintegrate as survival mode kicks in. What happens when there is no sudden, all encompassing catastrophe like Hurricane Katrina? What happens when there is a life of uncertainty and starvation to contend with on a daily basis? That social disintegration still takes place but it's not so overt. It's done on the street corner and back alleys. A willingness to sell destructive drugs to people in your community to people who look like you and share the same struggles as you. You understand the damage being caused but you also know you have to eat. The pervading thought is that you do what you have to do to survive.

Sociologists and other observers have studied this phenomenon for years. The data is available to anyone with a desire to access it. It is no coincidence that our drug laws takes away every safety net that an offender has so that he has no choice but to return to selling drugs as a means of support. Remember, when our laws make no sense to us it's usually the case that there is some special interest group with unlimited funds that has a lot to gain.

POLICE STATE

Chapter 11

In January of 2011, Camden cut it's police force almost in half due to budget cuts. 168 police officers and 67 firefighters were laid off. As you would expect, the crime rate went through the roof. Because people accept extreme measures in what they deem to be extreme times.the new Camden County Metro Police took over patrols in April of 2013. There was mixed reactions from the community. Some people were so tired of the murders and other crime until they felt anything would be an improvement. Other residents questioned what would happen when an almost entirely new police force, unfamiliar with Camden or it's residents, took over policing duties.

I had mixed feelings about it. I felt that something needed to be done because the violence had spiraled out of control. Out of eight nephews, four of them had been shot over the years. At the same time I had concerns about losing regular officers and replacing them with people unfamiliar with the city. Cops on the existing force had to apply for positions on the new force.

Not only had the faces of our police officers changed so had the city's landscape. Camden now has 120 surveillance cameras and 35 microphones that act as gun shot sensors all throughout the city. There are license plate readers that can scan dozens of plates every second. Downtown, at the Walter Rand Transportation Center, there is a 30 foot mobile cranes called Sky Patrol. As a result, the city has now earned the nickname, *Surveillance City*. The ACLU and other civil liberties groups have voiced concerns but to no avail.

One of the measures that residents initially welcomed was increased foot patrols. A noticeable police presence was sure to make an impact on crimes being committed. Foot patrols became problematic when Metro began just randomly stopping residents demanding them to produce an ID. It hasn't been limited to those engaged in illegal activity but to just about anyone who happens by.

On a September 26, 2014 segment of NBC Nightly News, reporter by Brian Williams, broadcast live from Camden. As he spoke, the cameraman panned the Metro officers standing in formation. It showed quite a few officers of color. I believe if you were to ask most residents they'd tell you that they haven't been seeing too many minority officers on the street. In a city that is 95% Black and Hispanic it would be interesting to know the racial breakdown of Metro officers.

Brian Williams reported that murders are down 53% in the city, with overall crime also decreasing by 21%.. At first glance the numbers are encouraging. Finally, Camden residents can begin to live in peace without fear. In reality, they've traded fear of drug dealers for fear of the police. Where they used to be able to avoid high drug areas and the violence associated with it, Metro does not allow residents the option of avoiding them. They patrol where they want to patrol. You are at risk of having your rights violated at any time and anywhere within the city limits.

There has definitely been a frightening trend in many communities across America, Camden included, of militarizing the local police force. It has become so problematic that President Obama has ordered a review of how the federal government gives local police departments military equipment including tanks, semi-automatic weapons and military style clothing. Granted, I'm not aware of any such equipment being distributed in Camden, however, it appears that Metro has certainly adopted the mentality. The mentality is an "Us-vs-Them" mindset. This thinking has officers conditioned to treat citizens as enemy combatants in a hostile territory. Much like soldiers in Vietnam or Iraq, "Camden's suburban soldiers" often can't make the distinction between who is friend or foe, a criminal or law abiding citizen. Make no mistake about it, there are definitely "boots on the ground" in Camden.

To say that there is growing tension and mistrust between US communities and some in law enforcement would be an understatement. U.S. Attorney General Eric Holder, in speaking of the shooting of Michael Brown in Fergueson, MO, wrote,

"This trust is all-important, but it is also fragile. It requires that force be used in appropriate ways. Enforcement priorities and arrest patterns must not lead to disparate treatment under the law, even if such treatment is unintended. And police forces should reflect the diversity of the communities they serve," he wrote.

He said it is *"painfully clear"* more progress, dialogue and action is needed on this issue in cities across the country. http://www.cbsnews.com/news/eric-holder-promises-full-and-fair-investigation-in-ferguson/

To place local officers with this militaristic view into local communities is a disaster waiting to happen. It's not difficult to make the leap considering the vast majority of the Metro Police are not from Camden and only know about Camden from things they've read or heard. Stories of police harassment have increased significantly. It's not uncommon to hear of residents being questioned and asked for ID. Officers seem to make no distinction about who gets stopped, men or women. Residents in cars, on foot or on bike. It doesn't matter. People I spoke with seem most angry about older residents being stopped and questioned. The following is a story from The Courier Post written by a Camden resident:

RABBLE ROUSER: Police intimidate Camden residents

"It has been one year since officers from the Camden County Police Department's Metro Division started their beat in Camden. To be perfectly honest, I can't say I feel any safer as a city resident.

Over the last year, I have witness so much wrongdoing by the Metro police.

'Harassment,' you can call it.

Never in my life have I witnessed so many men being required to sit on the curb of the sidewalks because the Metro police are conducting a car search. Witnessing so much of this day-after-day on certain streets in Camden is sickening.

The Camden County Metro Police style of policing is very intimidating."

I've witnessed first hand the fear and intimidation that comes with this para-military style of policing. For a city that is just coming into it's own, it must be disheartening for residents to be harassed by the very people brought in to help them. The Courier Post article continues:

"Prior to the Metro police taking form in Camden, I was very comfortable with the Camden City Police Department. Officers were always there when I needed them the most."

I've heard very similar stories from countless family and friends. A family member recalls sitting on a step on a main street in Parkside eating during his lunch break. Metro came up and demanded ID from him along with a line of young Black and Hispanic men. He made the mistake of thinking that he was free to sit outside and eat a hoagie during his lunch break. Perhaps he could have gotten away with that someplace else in America but not under the ever watchful eye of Big Brother in Camden.

This same relative had been sitting on the steps with his cousin when they saw Metro doing patrols. This time, so as not to antagonize officers with their presence, they stepped inside of a local establishment. Metro followed them inside, dragged them out and slammed them against the concrete. They were both asking the officers what they had done and the response they received was that they looked suspicious. When they were searched and nothing was found the officers moved on to their next target never apologizing and never looking even bothering to look back.

The idea of Camden Metro being in place to protect and serve has been called into question. I think it necessary to make it clear that I am not anti-police. Quite the contrary, I thank God for them. Having been born and raised in Camden, I can think of more than one occasion where they were a sight for sore eyes. In fact, when I was young, there were some police officers that we looked up to and had great respect for. Officer Lenny Hall would lecture you in such a way as to make you feel ashamed of even the thought of committing a crime. He died this year and the outpouring of grief was tremendous. He just passed a few months ago and the outpouring of grief by the

Camden community, both law abiding and criminal, was a real testament to his life. Mr. Thor is another Camden cop that greatly impacted the city's youth. At one time he even taught karate to neighborhood kids. I'm sure it was a tool to help keep them out of trouble. Trenton, NJ also had men in law enforcement that kids looked up to. Lieutenant James is a Trenton native who works at Mercer County Jail who often organizes fairs and fun-fests for the kids in Trenton. I am in no way saying that Metro police need to reach out to the community to the extent that the above men have but I'm trying to make the point that law enforcement can do their official duty while engaging community residents and not alienating them. It is possible to do both.

You may be thinking to yourself, "well…that's a problem for Camden but not for my community." Rest assured that with such a huge decrease in crime, I guarantee that this model used in Camden will be adopted elsewhere. In fact, Chief Thompson stated that he borrowed ideas from different police districts including New York. As soon as I started hearing story after story of Camden Metro stopping people New York immediately popped in my head. I can remember one story in particular of a young, black man who had been stopped dozens of times since stop and frisk laws took effect. In spite of protests by community activists and the ACLU this initiative was deemed very successful especially from a public relations stand point. Times Square was even compared to Disney Land because crime has dropped so dramatically. Thankfully, New York has made the decision to drop this racist practice.

"New York City will settle its long-running legal battle over the Police Department's practice of stopping, questioning and often frisking people on the street — a divisive issue at the heart of the mayoral race last year — by agreeing to reforms that a judge ordered in August, Mayor Bill de Blasio announced on Thursday.

In making the announcement, which he said he hoped would end a turbulent chapter in the city's racial history, Mr. de Blasio offered a sweeping repudiation of the aggressive policing practices that had been a hallmark of his predecessor, Michael R. Bloomberg, but that had stoked anger and resentment in many black and Latino neighborhoods. He essentially reversed the course set by Mr. Bloomberg, whose administration had appealed the judge's ruling. 'We're here today to turn the page on one of the most divisive problems in our city,' Mr. de Blasio said at a news conference. *'We believe in ending the overuse of stop-and-frisk that has unfairly targeted young African-American and Latino men.'* http://www.nytimes.com/2014/01/31/nyregion/de-blasio-stop-and-frisk.html?_r=0

I am not trying to take away from the fact that crime is down. In fact, I have been hoping and praying for this very kind of turn around for a long time. I'm just trying to make the point of "at what cost?" Before Metro took over residents knew what areas to stay away from to avoid the possibility of being victimized. Granted, this was not always foolproof. This method did not ensure 100% safety but neither can Camden Metro . People could come and go as they pleased. They could walk down the street without being harassed. There was no concern or second thoughts about making a quick run out of the house without bringing an ID.

Proponents of this blatant violation of civil rights will say, "they should be happy someone finally got the crime rate down so they must be stopping the criminals." Yes, they are stopping criminals but they are also stopping mothers, fathers, students, the elderly, visitors just passing through and everyone else in between. This would be the equivalent to a fireman running to the aid of a homeowner whose pot on the stove has caught fire. Instead of targeting the source of the problem and concentrating his efforts to the stove or even just to the kitchen, instead, the fireman has called in reinforcements all of whom have aimed their hoses to every part of the house and let the water go full blast. Everything in the house was ruined as a result. Was that fireman successful?

Yes, he can be considered a success in the sense that the fire on the stove has been put out. He is not a success in the sense that, in so doing, he has destroyed an entire home, the very thing he was called in to save and protect. Surely, the members of that household do not feel that it was worth losing everything they held dear. The members of that home are not against firemen. They are against the methods that that the firemen chose to use to put out that fire on the stove that cost them their beloved home. Yes, the home wasn't perfect. It needed repairs. It wasn't as nice as some of the other homes but it was still their home.

Camden residents may have a decrease in crime but surely it is at the cost of their freedom. Not only theirs but that of their family as well. I can remember reading stories about people in other countries who had limited freedom. They had to give an account of their every move. They were afraid of government authorities. They knew that their children also were subject to this same kind of constant surveillance and harassment. Prior to the end of the cold war, people in East Berlin desperately tried to cross the Berlin Wall reach West Berlin to get to freedom. In 1989 the wall finally came down amidst celebration and tears of joy.

Here it is 2014 and Camden NJ now has an invisible wall up. For poor and low-income residents who don't have the option to move they are just as much stuck behind that wall of poverty as much as any East Berliner had been prior to the wall coming down. Camden's wall even comes with surveillance towers that is reminiscent of the guard towers erected above the Berlin Wall. As Camdenites endure this, the world looks on, seeming not to care.

Diplomat, reporter and author, Carl T. Rowan wrote, *"It is often easier to become outraged by injustice half a world away than by oppression and discrimination half a block from home."*

It's not difficult to predict what will inevitably happen. Those who are able to move will do just that. There are still many hardworking people in Camden who are there as a matter of choice. How long will they be willing to stick with the decision to stay if they and their loved ones are continually subjected to harassment? What of the embarrassment they must feel when their family and friends who are visiting are subjected to the same treatment? Visits to the home will become less and less.

Not many people would be willing to stay in an area where they and their loved ones are subject to abusive treatment day in and day out, even though they've committed no crime. Simply because they are Camden residents they must have their ID on hand at all times. Of course, as the exodus from Camden increases, the already meager tax revenue to the city will decrease.

It had been suggested to me that people from Camden should not police or monitor other people from Camden. It's as if Camden residents can't be trusted to police themselves. Is it that they are more prone to being soft on criminals or more prone to corruption? Does it have something to do with their intellect or their ability to carry out the duties of a police officer in their native city?

Well, what do you know? In April of 2013 we see it happen right before our eyes….the replacements for Camden's police force are now predominately young, white and suburban. Apparently, the thought that we need outsiders come in and keep the peace was a little more widespread than I thought.

PIC (THE PRISON INDUSTRIAL COMPLEX)

Chapter 12

According to Wikepedia the Prison Industrial Complex is defined as: *"interest groups that represent organizations that do business in correctional facilities who are believed to be more concerned with making more money than actually rehabilitating criminals or reducing crime rates."* Our current justice system could actually be likened to an assembly line. Keeping production and profits up while keeping costs down is and must be the primary goal of any for profit business, otherwise, it would not be in business for long. The way to get this done is through our justice system. This should come as no surprise as it has always been the case that when the wealthy and others in power wanted to target a group of people to meet their needs, they simply created laws through which to work to obtain their goals. In his book, America's Courts and The Criminal Justice

System, David W. Neubauer writes, "*Historians suggest that medical or scientific knowledge about the harm of drugs has never played a significant role in formulating US drug policy. Rather, US policy has been driven by the desire to control groups considered threats to the existing social order.*" Thus, the Harrison Narcotics Act of 1914 targeted opium (used by Chinese in California), marijuana (smoked by Mexican Americans in the Southwest), and cocaine (allegedly being used by African Americans in the South)."

Of course these laws are always made to look as if they were designed with the good of society in mind or even that of the target group. While this may be the case sometimes, often public law and policy are driven by the agenda of special interest groups and negotiated by the powerful lobbyists that they hire. Camden's policy on drug possession within 1000 feet of a school zone is one such example. The following is an excerpt from the NJ Commission to Review Criminal Sentencing (2005):

"*The statistics bear out beyond doubt that the drug-free zone laws, as presently applied, have had a devastatingly disproportionate impact on New Jersey's minority community.*

"...New Jersey's cities are among the most densely populated in the nation. Given the large concentration of schools in these areas, the protective zones which surround them have overlapped and coalesced to such an extent that the three cities studied by the Commission – Jersey City, Camden, and Newark – have themselves become all encompassing drug free zones. The foregoing "urban effect" of the drug free zone laws significantly increases the likelihood that a drug distribution offense will occur within a drug free school zone in urban areas; minorities, who currently comprise a greater proportion of urban populations than rural and suburban populations, are therefore far more likely to be charged with a drug free zone offense and subjected to harsher punishment upon conviction. The unintended, but profoundly discriminatory, impact of the laws is the direct result of the size of the zones defined by the school zone and park zone laws, and is, moreover, significantly amplified by New Jersey's unique demographic characteristics.

The end result of this cumulative 'urban effect' of the drug free zone laws is that nearly every offender (96%) convicted and incarcerated for a drug free zone offense in New Jersey is either Black or Hispanic."

"A conviction for this crime is considered separate and distinct from all other drug-related offenses and will not merge with them. This means you will likely face two charges: one for distribution and one for distribution in a school zone. As such, you could face higher fines, more time behind bars, and parole ineligibility. In most cases, being convicted of violating N.J.S.A. 2C:35-7 is a third degree crime.

Camden is a city that is only 9 square miles and has 28 schools within it's borders.. It's virtually impossible not to be within 1000 feet of a school zone at any given time. I grew up in the city's Parkside section. From my street I was within 1000 feet of 4 schools: Hatch Middle School, Parkside Elementary School, Forrest Hill Elementary and Camden High. To give you some perspective, 1000 feet is the length of 3 football fields, the Eiffel Tower, which stands at 986 feet and 3 Empire State Buildings, each one standing at 305 feet. Also, keep in mind that the 1,000 feet is from any and all directions of the school, it's parking lot, or it's playground. What makes this statute worse is the fact that it has not been shown to be a deterrent from selling drugs. Thankfully, in January 2010, Governor Christie amended the Drug Free School Zone law to give judges discretion to waive or reduce mandatory terms.

School to Prison Pipeline

Not even children are safe from this ever-hungry money making machine called PIC. Increasingly, laws are being written that set our youngsters up for eventual placement into the correctional system. In the U.S. there are currently 2.7 million kids who have a parent in jail (http://www.justicefellowship.org/node/91). As you would expect from any child whose family has been torn apart there is sometimes acting out behavior which of course feeds the school-to-prison pipeline.

"The school to prison pipeline is a disturbing national trend wherein children are funneled out of public schools and into the juvenile and criminal justice systems. Many of these children have learning disabilities or histories of poverty, abuse or neglect, and would benefit from additional educational and counseling services. Instead, they are isolated, punished and pushed out."

"Zero-tolerance' policies criminalize minor infractions of school rules, while cops in school lead to students being criminalized for behavior that should be handled inside the school. Students of color are especially vulnerable to push-out trends and the discriminatory application of discipline."

https://www.aclu.org/school-prison-pipeline.

When school districts adopt such policies this begins a vicious cycle that ultimately leads to young black men being used for cheap or slave labor.

PRIVATIZING PRISONS

There has been a recent trend in corrections of privatizing jails and prisons. For profit companies have a vested interest in having more people locked up because it adds to their bottom line. These businesses have shareholders to answer to.

So what happens when the bottom line competes with justice? As is often the case, the bottom line wins. According to a September 19, 2013 *Huffington Post* article most of these businesses have quotas that mandate at least 90% of beds in prisons be filled. Consequently, if these quotas arent met then local and state governments have to pay a penalty fee in the millions of dollars. Hows that for incentive to lock up as many people as possible?

In 2011, a Pennsylvania judge was convicted of a "kids for cash" scheme. According to a February 21, 2011 ABC News article, Judge Mark Ciavarella accepted $1 million kickback from a private detention center in exchange for sending kids to their facility. The report goes on to say that children as young as 10 were incarcerated. One young man was sentenced to two years detention for joyriding in his mother's car. What will happen in our communities as this hungry monster seeks to be continually fed with fresh inmates, no matter how petty their crime? Will political leaders in these struggling communities be able to turn down the millions of dollars that they are offered for these contracts?

Many traditional mainstream American companies are involved in PIC. They sell goods to the complex or they have their goods produced by inmates in the complex greatly reducing their overhead. Everyday small businesses have a hard time competing with this behemoth. We need to keep in mind that these companies that are profiteering from inmate labor have Boards of Directors to report to. They absolutely must produce a profit or go out of business. American's are unknowingly buying goods produced by what can be described as slave labor. People are unaware that their hard earned money is supporting the oppression of a significant portion of the population.

"Private prisons are the biggest business in the prison industry complex. About 18 corporations guard 10,000 prisoners in 27 states. The two largest are Correctional Corporation of America (CCA) and Wackenhut, which together control 75%. Private prisons receive a guaranteed amount of money for each prisoner, independent of what it costs to maintain each one. According to Russell Boraas, a private prison administrator in Virginia, "the secret to low operating costs is having a minimal number of guards for the maximum number of prisoners." The CCA has an ultra-modern prison in Lawrenceville, Virginia, where five guards on dayshift and two at night watch over 750 prisoners. In these prisons, inmates may get their sentences reduced for "good behavior," but for any

infraction, they get 30 days added – which means more profits for CCA. According to a study of New Mexico prisons, it was found that CCA inmates lost 'good behavior time' at a rate eight times higher than those in state prisons."

http://www.globalresearch.ca/the-prison-industry-in-the-united-states-big-business-or-a-new-form-of-slavery/8289

PRISON REFORM

Chapter 13

It is no longer sustainable for state and local governments to house low level, non violent offenders. Prison reform is no longer optional, it's a necessity. Initially, the lobbyists and lawyers for PIC had their every wish granted to them by politicians who used their campaign contributions to win elections. These sweetheart deals that benefitted no one but those at the very top has now proven to be a money pit. Inmates have become much more expensive as they are becoming older and sicker. Healthcare costs for inmates have soared. Musician and songwriter, Frank Zappa rightly said, *"The illusion of freedom will continue as long as it's profitable to continue the illusion. At the point where the illusion becomes too expensive to maintain, they will just take down the scenery, they will pull back the curtains, they will move the tables and chairs out of the way and you will see the brick wall at the back of the theater."*

State and local governments, like New Jersey, are finding out just how unsustainable the current rate of incarceration is. It is decimating budgets all over the country. *"Since 2000, the number of prisoners over age 50 in New Jersey's state prisons has jumped nearly 90 percent. Now nearly 3,000 older prisoners are in the states eight adult correctional institutions.*

The older prisoner population has continued to soar even as the number of adult offenders incarcerated in New Jersey state prisons has declined by 7 percent since 2009, to about 17,000 last year, according to state Department of Corrections figures.

Older prisoners are also the fastest growing segment of the U.S. prison population. An estimated 246,000 people over 50 were behind bars last year, according to a 2012 American Civil Liberties Union report.

The growing number of older prisoners, like Thomas, represents a potential fiscal time bomb for the state and nation: Elderly prisoners cost more because almost all expenses related to their health care must be borne by state tax dollars."

http://www.nj.com/news/index.ssf/2013/03/upswing_in_aging_prison_inmate.html

We lead the world in incarcerating our own citizens. The US accounts for only 5% of the world's population but 25% of the world's prison population with 2 million inmates. The vast majority of inmates are African American and Hispanic. This country incarcerates more people than Russia and Communist China which has a population four times bigger than the US.

"Criminologists and legal scholars in other industrialized nations say they are mystified and appalled by the number and length of American prison sentences. Far from serving as a model for the world, contemporary America is viewed with horror," James Q. Whitman, a specialist in comparative law at Yale, wrote last year in Social Research. "Certainly there are no European governments sending delegations to learn from us about how to manage prisons."

"Prison sentences here have become vastly harsher than in any other country to which the United States would ordinarily be

compared," Michael H. Tonry, a leading authority on crime policy, wrote in The Handbook of Crime and Punishment.

http://www.nytimes.com/2008/04/23/us/23prison.html?pagewanted=all&_r=0

As the world looks on and as the costs of incarceration continue to increase prison reform was inevitable. Any number of initiatives have been helpful in decreasing the rate of incarceration for Camden's poor. As previously mentioned, drug court provides an alternative to lengthy prison sentences for drug offenders.

The mission of drug courts is to stop the abuse of alcohol and other drugs and related criminal activity. Drug courts are a highly specialized team process within the existing Superior Court structure that addresses nonviolent drug-related cases. They are unique in the criminal justice environment because they build a close collaborative relationship between criminal justice and drug treatment professionals.

The drug court judge heads a team of court staff, attorneys, probation officers, substance abuse evaluators and treatment professionals who work together to support and monitor a participant's recovery. They maintain a critical balance of authority, supervision, support and encouragement.

http://www.judiciary.state.nj.us/drugcourt/

In 2008, Fugitive Safe Surrender allowed people with warrants to come turn themselves in without threat of arrest. I had friends and family members who nervously took advantage of this opportunity. It wasn't easy as many weren't sure if this wasn't a ploy to get a large number of fugitives all at once. They took the risk and it paid off.

Operation Fugitive Safe Surrender was a partnership between The US Marshals and Antioch Baptist Church in Camden. People with warrants were allowed to turn themselves in without penalty. The initiative was a huge success. Organizers expected between 700 to 800 people to come. Instead 2,245 people showed up. Camden residents, and yes…that includes fugitives too, want to conform to the law and lead better lives just like anyone else. Look at the outcome when they're given half a chance.

http://www.usmarshals.gov/safesurrender/camden.htm

A BRIGHT FUTURE

Chapter 14

Many inmates and ex-offenders have sold themselves short. They've bought into the lie that what they have done is all that they will ever do. Often, hidden within such predictions is pure and unadulterated racism. The true underlying thought is you're not bright enough or capable enough to do anything more. You don't have the capability to make anything of your life. You will spend your life being told what to do. There are people who like to see young black and Hispanic men locked up in their prime. If they're in jail then they aren't reproducing and their free or nearly free labor also increases profits.

So many have believed the hype. They are totally convinced that a change in their lifestyle is not an option. I challenge those still in an institution to take notice of the inventive ways that they and other inmates have developed to cope and survive their incarceration.

Some time ago inmates at Camden Jail had developed a form of communication that had been used for years. It's a type of jailhouse sign language. This was developed by inmates to speak not only to each other but also to friends and family who stand outside of the jail and sign to them at the window. This was a quick, convenient way to talk to loved ones who were locked up without having to spend 2 hours in the waiting area for a 20 minute visit.

Years ago the jail had to blacken the windows because inmates were signing to people on the outside to tell them what car belonged to what correction officer, and then have them vandalize it. This was a temporary solution as inmates simply began to put white socks on their hands so people outside could still make out the message they were signing. Eventually, custody came up with a solution that stopped the signing for good. At one time, signing at Camden Jail was so well known in the Camden-Philadelphia area that it was featured on local news segments.

I've seen instances where having AIDS or claiming to have AIDS have offered inmates some level of protection from being attacked. One incident involved a female inmate at Mercer County Jail. She was petite inmate and cursed like a sailor. She didn't discriminate on who she let loose her verbal assault. After she had gotten people agitated and angry she would say "y'all b@#%! know I got AIDS!" No one attacked ever her either.

It's said that necessity is the mother of invention. People's innate need for survival and safety often produces creative solutions. Creative ability doesn't just disappear because you've changed environments. That same ability can be adapted to solve problems and create opportunities on the outside. It may be quite challenging at first because you're not used to it but, like anything else, you have to keep at it to succeed.

BUSINESS SAVY

Chapter 15

Many current and former inmates demonstrate a good business sense and would probably do well if given the chance. The sad fact is that many men and women would like to get out of the game and get a legitimate job but there are more barriers to this, now more than ever before. Having a criminal record is a huge challenge to overcome in even a good economy. Large gaps in employment history or very little employment history at all. Stiff competition from the community at large: college kids, seniors, laid off workers, etc.

Invariably, many in the drug game find themselves back in the same position that they promised never to return to again. Most of the people that I know who are in this business is in it as a means of economic survival. It's kind of hard for someone to hear, "dont start hustling," when they know that there is no food for them or their children. When someone they love are facing eviction. When their kids are being teased for not having any decent clothes or shoes. Situations like these factor into the decision to sell drugs instead of being staying broke.

In Camden County Jail a large percentage of inmates come from the inner city where there is a huge, thriving drug market. If there is any difficulty in getting a job it is much easier for these young people to make money selling drugs. Many of these drug sets have operations that rival legitimate businesses. There are managers, distributors, and line level staff who are involved in day to day sales Different areas are scouted and reviewed for the potential of opening a new market. There is the consideration of nearby competing markets. If this isn't the same as some established, brick and mortar retail business then I don't know what is.

Can you imagine the level of success these young men could have if they refused to accept the limitations put on them? Few of them have challenged their supposed designated roles in society. Feeling trapped and hopeless they believe this is the only "business sector" that has a place for them. If they continue to limit themselves to traditional jobs, which they've been locked out of, then they might be right.

In order to break out of these bonds they absolutely must begin to consider other options such as starting a business. Opening a stand. Selling items online. Offering a service such as home repairs, painting, or auto repairs. Consider signing up with a well established, reputable network marketing business. Some very successful, well known millionaires have stated that this is a great way to earn money without being employed at a traditional job. Both Donald Trump and Robert Kiyosaki, two great powerhouses in the business world, have done their own research on the subject. Not only do they feel that this is a viable way to earn a living they also stated that this form of business can be expected to grow a great deal in the near future. In fact, Robert Kiyosaki has written a book on the subject, "The Business Of The 21st Century."

I once worked as a private contractor for a well known agency in Philadelphia. I was telling my colleague about Robert Kiyosaki's book "Rich Dad Poor Dad" and the need for us to become more financially educated and eventually entrepreneurs. I had just finished reading it. Incredibly, her response was to brag that she had read the book more than 10 years ago. Her intent was to let me know that I was giving her old news. My thoughts were, "if you read this book 15 years ago why, are you still in the same financial position you've always been in?" She was working right along side me as a temporary Case Manager, a position which could end at any minute. Don't get me wrong, there is nothing wrong with temp work. In fact, I worked for years as a temp worker for Social Work PRN in Ft. Washington, Pa. The owner and staff really works hard to make sure that each contractor is well-equipped and best suited for the assignment they were given. This really helped me to grow in my career after I felt burnt out. It gave me the option of picking and choosing what assignments I would accept.

What I am saying is that" Rich Dad Poor Dad" was not a piece of fiction meant to be read for entertainment. For me, the book was a life changing call to action. I recommend this book to everyone; inmates, ex-inmates, single moms, and anyone who wants to take control of their financial future. Living in fear of losing a job or never finding a job is stressful and exhausting. It doesn't have to be that way. We all have something to offer the world.

The reason each of us are hardwired a certain way is because we've been created with specific abilities that address the needs of the community that no one else can do quite like us. We are all uniquely gifted individually but our gifts are to be used to benefit many people beyond ourselves and loved ones. Some are gifted teachers. Some are gifted writers. Some are gifted builders. Whatever the gift, we have to make use of it and share it. It's like a 1,000 piece puzzle. Each piece has a small part that reveals a complete picture when added to the other pieces. No other puzzle piece, no matter how similar, can perfectly fill the space the way the piece that it was designed for can.

The talent that I've seen flowing through the halls of Camden County Jail, Mercer County Jail and Kintock is mind-blowing. Fear. Insecurity. Misplaced belief in the negative labels put on them have all worked together to cause talented and gifted people to add limitations to themselves on top of the ones that society has already put on them. The good news is that it doesn't have to stay that way.

In Camden and other urban communities across the country there is often some level of resentment about some of the foreign business owners who come into the country and then set up shop in our neighborhood. There's been a long held belief that Korean merchants, in particular, are given an allotment of cash to get their businesses started. I honestly don't know if this is true or not but what I do know is that many people from other countries had no choice but to become entrepreneurs in their native countries because they have very limited government help to get on their feet (much like millions of minorities with drug charges here in our own country).

I'm not against any business owner coming into the community and doing business. I am against a business owner who comes from a culture where discrimination against darker-skinned people is practiced and tolerated and then the person sets up shop in Camden and treats the black residents with disdain because this is what they've become accustomed to doing. This is totally unacceptable. Unfortunately, I've seen it happen dozens of times.

When an entrepreneur from another country comes here, they must acclimate and observe the laws of their new adopted country, not vice versa. Keep in mind though, civil rights, affirmative action and the Equal Opportunity Commission is non- existent in many other countries. A store owner can't charge one price to a black person and a lower price to someone of their own race (unfortunately this has been known to happen in Camden). Nor can they treat other customers rudely because of their ethnicity. This may very well be the way business is conducted in their native land but it should not be incorporated into business practices here. It is up to us to challenge this. Add this to a growing list of reasons that more oppressed and disenfranchised groups need to open their own business.

As the job market locks more and more people out, we should all look for a way to ensure a living without limiting ourselves to looking for a job that may or may not ever come. If you are able to secure a traditional job, then by all means, do so. Just remember, you do have the option to take off the limitations placed on you, keep an open mind and consider being your own boss. Noted author, businessman and motivational speaker, T. Harv Eker summed it up best, *"it's simple arithmetic: your income can only grow to the extent that you do."*

There are resources in the city that offers assistance and/ or training to those looking to start their own business. The Camden Dream Center http://www.camdendreamcenter.org/ offers training and seminars for those seeking to start their own business. There is also a youth targeted program called Youth Entrepreneurship Series (Y.E.S) program. Started in 2010, YES is a partnership with Rutgers University School of Business. An entrepreneurship boot camp was held. There was a 90% completion rate of which 100% indicated an interest in owning their own business.

The Latin American Economic Development Association (LAEDA) http://www.laeda.com/ offers training to aspiring entrepreneurs. They are committed to the creation of small business ownership opportunities for all minorities. I know of several people who have gotten their businesses started through the training they received at LAEDA.

Even if a resident is on public assistance, they have the right to start a business and be allowed to do the things necessary to pursue. Thankfully, it's written right into the handbook for TANF clients. Keep in mind that the program that you are assigned to for your work activity will require proof of self employment as will Camden County Board of Social Services. It's well worth your time and energy to explore this option.

NOTABLE RESIDENTS

Chapter 16

I would like to emphasize that even with all of the challenges that Camden City faces many of it's residents still make it in spite of what they face on a daily basis. Beyond that, there are still more current and former residents who are doing amazing things to make a difference in the community. Often the question is asked, "Can anything good come from Camden?" This was the same exact question they asked about Jesus of Nazareth (John 1:45-46). Of course the answer is an emphatic, "YES!!!" The following is just a few Camden residents who are working to improve the quality of life in Camden…they're making a difference. I believe that we are witnessing the beginning of The Camden Renaissance!

Tawanda Jones is the founder of Camden Sophisticated Sisters Drill Team (http://camdensophisticatedsisters.org/). This woman has dedicated nearly 30 years of her life to providing young girls in

Camden City with a safe, nurturing place to go and participate in drill team. The talented young ladies on her team must keep their grades up if they want to remain in good standing with the team. At a time when a reported 49% of Camden students graduate from high school (http://www.cnn.com/2013/03/25/us/new-jersey-camden-schools/), she has managed to help her girls achieve a 100% graduation rate. Educators around the country should be banging her door down to find out how she does it. That is an amazing statistic. Tawanda has gained national recognition for her efforts and deservedly so. Her commitment and dedication are to be commended.

Made in Camden clothing store was founded by Artist and Entrepreneur, Anthony "Tone Lok" Dillard. He started a clothing line that's located on Haddon Ave in the Parkside section of the city. A self-admitted, former drug dealer who has served prison time, Dillard turned his life around. His story was of particular interest to me because this is an example of a young, black man from Camden who was used to making fast money. In no way has this ambition to generate revenue changed…now he makes money legitimately. He is his own boss. He still makes money on his own terms but now his income is not subject to forfeiture laws nor does it require the loss of his freedom.

Next is a young rap artist named Rashaan "Yung Poppa" Hornsby (http://www.yungpoppa.com/). Only 14 years old, this Camden native has taken it upon his self to use his gift of verse to fight bullying in Camden and elsewhere. This is an amazing achievement. Bullying has gotten so out of control that kids who have been targeted are choosing to kill themselves and sometimes other kids. Some of these beautiful babies are being tormented on the internet through social media.

Yung Poppa acts as a counterbalance to all of the madness. He has both the heart and talent to be a voice in the world of hip-hop and say bullying is not cool nor is it right. He is just as well known for his intellect as he is for his athletic prowess. Young people are so easily influenced by what the crowd is doing. Yung Poppa challenged the status quo and is using his influence to improve lives and not just his bank account. It takes a lot of heart to stand against the crowd...doing what everyone else is doing really would be the easiest thing to do. He is definitely a leader in the making.

Last, but not least is Chris Collins. He is CEO and Editor-In-Chief of Anointed News Journal (http://anointedonline.net/). Chris is originally from Camden and is a former school mate. He uses his paper to do what other media outlets have neglected to do...spotlight the positive people and organizations in Camden. He has spent his career publishing news that matters to us. This year Anointed News Journal celebrated its 19th year in publication. Congratulations to Chris and the rest of the Anointed News staff.

These current and former residents are stepping up to the plate and doing what needs to be done for the city. They aren't waiting for someone else to come in and make things happen. They saw a need and decided to address it. I had them and some other Camdenites in mind when I wrote the following monologue.

<u>Married to Camden</u>

Camden is like a husband you've loved for years that slowly began to change for the worse. He had become a shadow of his former self. The two of you grew in different directions. You sat by helpless, unsure what to do, as he started to decline. Everybody keeps telling you, "leave him." "You would do so much better with someone else." "He'll only hurt you in the long run." You defend him saying, "he's a really good man and he didn't used to be like this."

You explain that your smaller kids are too young to remember what a great man their dad used to be. You hope and pray that his problems won't impact them…but…it eventually does. Reluctantly, you take your kids and leave the love of your life because their lives will be harder if you stay. Remembering when he first started going downhill you promised you wouldn't abandon him like so much of his family and friends had. You try to move on but you find yourself constantly checking the paper or watching the news hoping to hear anything even remotely related to him.

As usual, the reporter selectively focuses on his bad qualities but none of his good. Although you try not to…you get defensive. You and the rest of the family hate it when outsiders criticize him because they don't really know him or his potential. The good news is that several dedicated family members took decisive steps to get him back on his feet. They had to endure the negativity of his haters. "He's not worth it." "You just can't change some people." "He got help before and what good did it do?!"Camden's dedicated and capable sons and daughters politely answered them back without words but with action. Like the critics, Camden's own had also grown tired of failed promises to rehabilitate him, so instead, they just went to work. Without much money or publicity, at a very grassroots and local level, they used their talents to help rebuild their father and his reputation. Now when you look at him you can see glimpses of his former glory. You can admit it…he's looking pretty good. But you don't know if you can trust it. He's made changes before but it never lasted… but… the improvements are hard to ignore. Camden's family have come together and made changes everybody was hoping for.

PROGRESS

Chapter 17

It feels good to report on some very positive developments that are happening in Camden. The first new grocery store to open in Camden in 40 years, Price Rite, opened on October 15, 2014. Owners describe it as a cross between Aldi and Costco.

Also, the city of Camden has announced plans to demolish 600 abandoned properties. Mayor Dana Redd said that this would be the biggest demolition initiative ever undertaken in the state. She went on to say that this would send a clear message that the city is serious about improving it's neighborhoods.

The Philadelphia 76ers will be opening a new practice facility and office building at the city's waterfront. In return the organization will be receiving an $82 million tax break from the state to be spread over the next 10 years. Mayor Redd indicated that the move will cause a "spill-over effect" for other area businesses.

Finally, Holtec International, a power plant supplier, will build a manufacturing facility in Camden at the city's waterfront. It's expected to create 235 jobs. In return Holtec will receive $260 in tax credits. This is the biggest tax credit ever for NJ.

HELPING INMATES TRANSITION

Chapter 18

Like most other government institutions jails are struggling financially. To keep costs down administrators may have to cut programs that are beneficial to inmates. Jails are often more than willing to accept volunteers to help defray costs. People are needed to help inmates prepare for their GED. Perhaps you have some kind of skill or knowledge about a particular trade that you could share. Inmates would benefit from this greatly. If you play an instrument or sing you could arrange to perform at the jail. Be advised that administration will run a background check on anyone seeking to enter the jail. Several years ago a family friend was at Camden County Jail to apply for a job in the kitchen. She actually ended up as an inmate because there was a warrant out for her arrest.

If youre busy like most people are you could donate your books instead of your time. According to financial educator and guru, Robert Kiyosaki, "knowledge is the new money." If this is the case, and I agree that it is, then you could greatly improve not only their lives but inmates' earning potential as well. Especially helpful would be books related to self improvement. Text books, How To books, Faith inspired books and anything that would help people to learn, grow and use their time wisely. Because there is so much down time inmates are bored and hungry for knowledge. This is the perfect opportunity to help mold someone into the person they want to be by simply providing them the tool to do it. Much like in the community, books have the capacity to literally change lives. You could expose people to ideas and concepts totally foreign to them but helpful nonetheless.

Please refrain from offering books that don't add anything to the inmates' intellect or well being. No books on sex, drugs, or how to be a better criminal. It probably wouldn't get past security anyway as each book has to be inspected not only for contraband but also for appropriate content.

Whatever way you choose to get involved is an entirely personal decision that carries much more of an impact than you might think. We have the opportunity to not just be spectators, angry and appalled at what's going on around us, but to be active participants addressing society's problems. Even if the help you're able to offer is not benefitting the city of Camden, there are plenty of "little Camdens" all over the country where you can still make a difference. Perhaps you had been unaware of what millions of your oppressed, fellow Americans had to contend with. Now that you know what are you willing to do?

To be informed of upcoming projects and events please email us at:

CamdenEmpowered@gmail.com

www.ingramcontent.com/pod-product-compliance
Lightning Source LLC
Chambersburg PA
CBHW051725170526
45167CB00002B/798